TUSCANY TRAVEL GUIDE 2023:

A Complete And Essential Guide To Plan Your Trip To Tuscany, Insider's Secrets And Guide To The History, Art, Fashion, Food, Culture, Top Cities And Attractions In Tuscany.

Robert R. Hill

D1319566

1

Table Of Contents

FOREWORD

There was a young lady called Emily who had always wanted to go to Tuscany. She had grown up hearing tales of the rolling hills, lovely vineyards, and quaint towns that made up this enchanted part of Italy her Italian grandmother. She knew precisely where she wanted to go when she had finally collected enough money for a single international vacation.

It was a bright and beautiful morning when Emily arrived in Tuscany. Tourists and locals alike crowded into the airport, eager to see this stunning region of Italy's sights and sounds. Stepping outdoors into the fresh Italian air, Emily took a deep breath and felt her pulse beat with excitement.

In the little town of Greve, which is tucked away amid the Chianti region's rolling hills and vineyards, she had leased a modest apartment. Finding a decent cup of coffee and a croissant to start her day off correctly was Emily's first order of business. She walked through the village's winding, cobblestone streets until she came to a little café with patio seating. She placed an order for a coffee and a warm croissant, enjoying each mouthful.

Emily observed the sights and noises of the village as she sat there. The air was filled with the beautiful aroma of blossoming flowers and the perfume of freshly cooked bread. She felt the warm wind swish over her hair as the sun scorched her face. At that moment, she realized her journey to Tuscany would be much more amazing than she had anticipated.

The next few days were spent by Emily exploring the area, enjoying the mouthwatering cuisine and wine, as well as the breathtaking landscape. She traveled to Siena, an old city with magnificent Gothic architecture and twisting lanes that appeared to lead to obscure nooks and obscure passageways. She walked around Florence's marketplaces negotiating prices with sellers of handmade ceramics, leather products, and vibrant fabrics. She also visited the many vineyards and wineries that dot the landscape, where she learned about winemaking and indulged in some regional Chianti.

Emily concluded that her vacation to Tuscany had given her more than just memories as she sat outside her apartment and watched the sunset over the hills one evening. She now saw things from a different angle. She had discovered how to enjoy the present moment, appreciate the beauty of her surroundings, and form relationships with the individuals she encountered.

Emily was getting ready to depart Tuscany when she realized she would remember these teachings for the rest of her life. She would never forget the friendliness and kindness of the people she had encountered, the breathtaking scenery, or the sense of freedom and pleasure that had filled her heart while she had been in this magnificent place.

And so Emily kissed Tuscany goodbye and began her trip back home with a sorrowful heart but a spirit full of gratitude. She was certain that she would always cherish her travel experiences and that she would one day return to the charming area that had won her heart...

WELCOME TO TUSCANY

A gorgeous area of Italy, welcome to Tuscany! Tuscany provides tourists with a one-of-a-kind and enduring travel experience with its rolling hills, ancient villages, and food and wine of international renown.

See the area's numerous ancient cities, like Florence, Siena, and Pisa, which are home to some of the finest pieces of art and architecture in the world, as you travel through it. When you admire the works of Renaissance artists like Michelangelo, Leonardo da Vinci, and Botticelli, be sure to look up to the famed Leaning Tower of Pisa to take in the beautiful vistas.

The scenic landscape of Tuscany, which is filled with quaint towns and villages, is another feature of the region. Drive through the beautiful Chianti wine area to sip some of the best wines in the world and take in the breathtaking vistas of the vineyards and olive fields.

The cuisine of Tuscany, which is centered on fresh, locally produced ingredients and traditional traditions, is sure to please food enthusiasts. Enjoy meals like bistecca alla Fiorentina, a luscious grilled steak, and ribollita, a substantial vegetable soup. Don't forget to sample the region's renowned gelato, which is crafted with fresh fruit and creamy local milk.

In addition to its towns, landscape, and food, Tuscany is home to a variety of other worthwhile attractions. There are many thermal springs and spas in the area where you may unwind and revitalize in the mineral-rich waters.

Tuscany offers a wide variety of activities for outdoor lovers. Go for a walk in one of the breathtaking natural parks, such as Parco Naturale della Maremma or Parco delle Colline Metallifere, or ride a bike through the meadows and hills.

Visit the various museums and archaeological sites in Tuscany if you have an interest in history. You may visit the tombs, relics, and ruins left behind by the Etruscan culture, which predates the Roman Empire, all around Tuscany.

Last but not least, don't pass up the chance to go to one of Tuscany's many festivals or events. These festivals, which range from the Giostra del Saracino jousting competition in Arezzo to the Palio horse race in Siena, are a wonderful opportunity to explore the local customs and culture.

We wish you a wonderful stay in Tuscany as you explore everything that this wonderful area has to offer. And don't be afraid to ask the welcoming locals for assistance or advice while you're there; they're always delighted to share their passion for the area. Have a great time and safe travels!

CHAPTER 1: INTRODUCTION

History Of Tuscany

The central Italian region of Tuscany has a long and complicated history that dates back more than two thousand years. From ancient times, the area has been inhabited, and throughout history, it has been shaped by several civilizations, including the Etruscans, the Romans, and the medieval city-states. Italian politics, art, and culture have all benefited greatly from Tuscany's influence.

Prehistoric and Etruscan Period: The Paleolithic age, or around 200,000 years ago, is the oldest known period of human presence in Tuscany. Tuscany saw the emergence of the earliest agricultural villages during the Neolithic era (6000-4500 BC). Megalithic monuments, like the dolmens and menhirs discovered in the Lunigiana area, were left behind by these societies.

The Etruscans were a great civilization that inhabited Tuscany from the eighth to the third century BC. They left a lasting impression on the area's culture, architecture, and art. The Etruscans created magnificent cities as well as an advanced writing and religious system. They also created some of the most exquisite artwork and jewelry in antiquity. In the third century BC, the Etruscan civilization began to crumble, and Tuscany joined the Roman Empire.

Roman Period: Tuscany was crucial to the economic and cultural growth of the Roman Empire from the third century BC to the fifth century AD. The area was well recognized for its agriculture, particularly for the wine and olive oil it produced. The Roman amphitheater in Lucca and the hot baths in Saturnia are only two of the many Roman palaces and structures that were constructed in Tuscany.

Middle Ages: Tuscany was split into several city-states throughout the Middle Ages, including Firenze, Siena, and Pisa. They produced some of the best writers, thinkers, and architects of their day, and these city-states were well-known for their political, economic, and cultural significance. Several strong feudal rulers, such as the Counts of Guidi and the Counts of Tuscany, made Tuscany their home.

Tuscany became a hub of the European textile trade in the eleventh century, with towns like Florence and Lucca becoming significant textile makers. This resulted in the emergence of a prosperous merchant elite that fostered the development of humanism, a cultural movement that highlighted the value of human reason and individuality, as well as becoming patrons of the arts.

Renaissance: Tuscany developed into a hub of creative and cultural innovation throughout the Renaissance era (14th–16th centuries) when some of the most well-known works by artists like Leonardo da Vinci, Michelangelo, and Botticelli were produced. The Medici family, which controlled Florence from the 15th to the 18th century, was a significant patron of the arts and helped the Renaissance and the growth of humanism.

Moreover, Tuscany was crucial to the growth of Italian politics. After the French invasion of Italy in 1494, Naples' Charles VIII was anointed king. As a result, there was political unrest in Tuscany for a while as several groups fought for control. The Medici family retook control of Florence in

1512, and they quickly put in place a reliable administration that lasted until the 18th century.

Modern Era: Tuscany joined the Kingdom of Italy in the 19th century, and Florence was selected as the nation's new capital. Several Tuscan academics and politicians supported the fight for Italian independence, which played a significant part in the unification of Italy.

Tuscany was controlled by the Germans during World War II and saw intense warfare between the Allies and the Axis forces. Significant damage was done to the area, and several historic structures and items of art were destroyed. During the war, Tuscany went through a period of fast economic and social growth. Several businesses there grew, and the area saw a rise in tourism.

Tuscany is renowned today for its stunning scenery, storied towns, and rich cultural history. The ancient capitals of Florence, Siena, and Pienza, as well as the Val d'Orcia and the Medici

Villas and Gardens, are among the numerous UNESCO World Heritage sites in the area. Tuscany is renowned for its culinary and wine traditions, with many well-known foods and beverages coming from the area.

In conclusion, Tuscany's long history dates back more than two millennia and has been influenced by several civilizations and cultural currents. Tuscany has been a significant contributor to the growth of Italian art, culture, and politics from the prehistoric and Etruscan through the Roman, Middle Ages, Renaissance, and contemporary times. Tuscany is still a thriving, dynamic area with a rich history, culture, and natural beauty.

Art And Architecture

The world has benefited from the cultural and architectural accomplishments of Tuscany, a region in central Italy. From the early Etruscan period until the Renaissance, Tuscany has always been a center of artistic innovation. We shall go into great depth about the art and architecture of Tuscany in this article.

Tuscany- Art Style

Some of the most important pieces of art in the world have their origins in Tuscany. The ancient Etruscans, who lived in the area between the eighth and third centuries BC, are responsible for the development of local art. The Etruscans have accomplished metalworkers, and their artwork was distinguished by complex patterns and expert workmanship. Greek art had a significant effect on Etruscan art, which often included images from myths.

Tuscany was a major center for religious art throughout the Middle Ages, with several churches and monasteries commissioning pieces to decorate their walls. The paintings by Cimabue at the Basilica of San Francesco in Assisi from the 13th century are among the most outstanding specimens of medieval art in

Tuscany. Among the best specimens of early Italian Renaissance painting, these murals show incidents from the life of St. Francis of Assisi.

In Tuscany, the Renaissance was a time when art flourished. Tuscany was the home to some of the greatest artists in history, including Leonardo da Vinci, Michelangelo, and Raphael. The Renaissance was founded in Florence, the capital of Tuscany, and many of the most important pieces of art from this period may be found there.

Michelangelo's David is among the most recognizable pieces of Renaissance art in Tuscany. One of the best sculptures ever made is the statue, which features the biblical figure, David. The monument took Michelangelo four years to finish after it was given to him by the city of Florence in 1501. The David is presently kept at Florence's Accademia Gallery and is regarded as one of the city's must-see sights.

Leonardo da Vinci's The Last Supper, which is housed at the Convent of Santa Maria delle Grazie in Milan, is another well-known piece of Renaissance art in Tuscany. The artwork is evidence of Tuscany's impact on the Renaissance even though it was not created there. Leonardo da Vinci lived much of his time in Tuscany, and the creative movement was greatly impacted by his works.

Tuscany Architectural style

Some of the greatest architectural feats in history may be found in Tuscany. Each architectural period has left its stamp on the area, from Renaissance palaces to ancient Etruscan ruins.

Large-scale temples and tombs were among the great architectural achievements of the Etruscans. The Tomb of the Leopards in Tarquinia is one of Tuscany's most spectacular Etruscan monuments. Frescoes representing episodes from Etruscan mythology are used to embellish the tomb, which was built in the fourth century BC.

Tuscany was a major center for ecclesiastical architecture throughout the Middle Ages, and several churches and monasteries were built there. The Cathedral of Santa Maria del Fiore in Florence is one of Tuscany's most striking specimens of medieval architecture. The cathedral, which Filippo Brunelleschi planned and finished in the fifteenth century, is well-known for its enormous dome.

In Tuscany, the Renaissance was a period of remarkable architectural accomplishment when several palaces, churches, and public structures were

erected at this time. The Palazzo Vecchio in Florence is one of Tuscany's most important Renaissance structures. The palace, which was first built in the 14th century, underwent a 16th-century Renaissance-style makeover. Impressive frescoes, including those by Vasari and Michelangelo, can be seen throughout the Palazzo Vecchio.

The Palazzo Pitti in Florence is another magnificent Renaissance structure in Tuscany. The Medici dynasty eventually acquired the palace, which was first constructed in the 15th century for the Pitti family. Many museums and galleries, notably the Palatine Gallery and the Boboli Gardens, are now located within the palace, which was enlarged in the 16th and 17th centuries.

Tuscany is renowned for its magnificent fortifications and castles, which were built all across the area to stave against invaders. The Fortezza di Montalcino, one of Tuscany's most well-known strongholds, was constructed in the 14th century to protect the city of Montalcino. Nowadays, the stronghold houses a museum and is a well-liked tourist attraction.

Conclusion

Italy and the rest of the world have been forever changed by the art and architecture of Tuscany. Tuscany's art and architecture reflect the region's rich history and cultural legacy, from the prehistoric Etruscan ruins to the Renaissance palaces. The works of those who came before them had an impact on the artists and architects of the area, and they in turn had an impact on later generations of artists and architects.

People from all over the globe are still drawn to the art and architecture of Tuscany. Millions of people visit the area each year to marvel at the beauty and workmanship of Tuscany's creative and architectural accomplishments. These tourists travel to the region's museums, galleries, and architectural sites.

Customs And Culture

Tuscany is a region in central Italy renowned for its breathtaking scenery, extensive history, and dynamic culture. The area is home to several well-known cities, each with its cultural legacy, including Florence, Pisa, Siena, and Lucca.

The history and customs of Tuscany are profoundly ingrained in its culture. The area has a strong artistic tradition, and many of the most well-known pieces of art in the world may be found in its cities. The art and architecture of Florence, in particular, which is considered the cradle of the Renaissance, are examples of this artistic and architectural trend.

The Palio di Siena, a horse race that occurs twice a year in the city of Siena, is one of the most well-known cultural traditions of Tuscany. The race is a fiercely contested sport with a long history that stretches back to the 16th century. The race is entered by a horse and rider from each of the city's 17 contrades, and it is fiercely competitive. The winning district receives honors and a place in the annals of the city.

Tuscany is renowned for its food as well, which is centered on straightforward, seasonal ingredients and conventional cooking methods. Tuscan cuisine is often distinguished by its use of olive oil, bread, and wine, and dishes like bistecca alla Fiorentina (a grilled steak) and ribollita (a soup prepared with bread and vegetables) are well-liked throughout the area.

The music of Tuscany is a significant component of its culture. Both more modern musical genres and many traditional folk songs and dances are prevalent in the area. "Bella Ciao," a partisan song that was written during World War II and has since become a symbol of resistance and independence, is one of the most well-known songs from Tuscany.

Tuscany is renowned for its breathtaking scenery in addition to its artistic and cultural heritage. The area is home to the untamed Apennine

Mountains as well as undulating hills, vineyards, and olive orchards. Many tourists go to Tuscany to take in the area's natural beauty and discover its many cycling and hiking routes.

Another significant aspect of the area's cultural legacy is Tuscan architecture. Beautiful examples of Gothic and Renaissance architecture, such as the well-known Cathedral in Florence and the Leaning Tower of Pisa, may be seen in the towns of Florence, Pisa, and Siena.

The importance of religion in Tuscan culture is further shown by the abundance of stunning cathedrals and churches in the area. One of the most well-known churches in the world is Florence's Duomo, which houses magnificent creations by Renaissance masters like Michelangelo, Donatello, and others.

Tuscany is renowned for its festivals and festivities in addition to its extensive artistic and cultural legacy. The Carnevale di Viareggio, a carnival held in the seaside town of Viareggio, is one of the most well-known. The festival draws thousands of tourists from all over the globe and is known for its extravagant floats, costumes, and parades.

The Festa della Rificolona, which takes place in Florence on September 7th, is another significant event in Tuscany. The celebration is based on an old custom when farmers would transport lanterns to Florence to market their wares. A procession of lanterns and other events are part of the celebration today.

Also well-known for its wine, Tuscany is home to some of Italy's most renowned vineyards. Tuscan wines, which include well-known types like Chianti, Brunello di Montalcino, and Vino Nobile di Montepulciano, are renowned for their complexity and richness. Tuscan cuisine emphasizes wine, and many eateries and trattorias in the area have comprehensive wine lists with regional selections.

The idea of "la belle figura," which roughly translates to "the lovely figure," is another significant component of the Tuscan culture. This idea, which is mirrored in the clothes, design, and general aesthetic of the area, stresses the need of conducting oneself in a polished and refined way.

Tuscan clothing is distinguished by its timeless designs, premium fabrics, and traditional, exquisite aesthetic. Tuscany is the birthplace of several well-known Italian fashion designers, like Gucci and Roberto Cavalli, and the area is home to a large number of boutique stores and fashion businesses.

Tuscan style is renowned for its natural materials, including terra cotta, stone, and wood, as well as its rustic elegance. Traditional architectural features seen in many Tuscan houses and structures include terracotta roofs, wooden shutters, and wrought-iron details.

Tuscany is famed for its agricultural background, and its culture is closely tied to the soil. Wheat, olives, grapes, sunflowers, and other crops are among the many products grown by Tuscan farmers. Throughout Tuscany, several farms and wineries provide agritourism opportunities, letting guests taste regional goods and learn about traditional agricultural practices.

The idea of "slow food" plays a significant role in Tuscan culture and cuisine. Slow eating highlights the value of utilizing seasonal, locally sourced foods and conventional cooking techniques. In Tuscany, many eateries and trattorias specialize in slow cuisine and have menus with traditional Tuscan meals and fresh, straightforward ingredients.

Lastly, the Tuscan culture places a high value on family and community. The area is renowned for having a strong feeling of community, and several towns and villages celebrate and organize traditional festivities that unite people. The importance of family is also very important in Tuscan culture, and many families have resided there for many generations.

In conclusion, Tuscany's history, artistic legacy, breathtaking scenery, and thriving villages all play a significant role in the region's culture and customs. Tuscany is a place with something for everyone, from its renowned art and architecture to its delectable food, lovely fashion, and focus on family and community.

Landscapes And Nature

With its undulating hills, vast vineyards, and picture-perfect towns and villages, Tuscany is renowned for its magnificent natural beauty. Tuscany provides an impressive variety of natural scenery, from the rough Tyrrhenian Sea shoreline to the breathtaking peaks of the Apennine Alps.

Hills that are covered with vineyards, olive groves, sunflowers, and wheat fields, and vineyards dominate the area. Several of Tuscany's well-known towns and cities, such as Florence, Siena, and Pisa, have a spectacular background provided by the hills. Many little hamlets and towns may be found among the undulating hills, many of which still preserve their original beauty and character.

The Val d'Orcia, a magnificent valley that spans from the hills south of Siena to Mount Amiata, is one of Tuscany's most well-known landscapes. The valley is renowned for its breathtaking views of the surrounding hills, cypress trees, and several ancient villages and castles. Because of the unique combination of natural and cultural beauty in the Val d'Orcia, it has been named a UNESCO World Heritage Site.

The Chianti area of Tuscany is another well-known scenery because of its vineyards and gently undulating hills covered with cypress and olive groves. Several of Tuscany's well-known wineries, which provide some of Italy's best wines, are located in this area. The Chianti area is renowned for its charming hamlets and villages, many of which were built during the Middle Ages.

Another notable feature of Tuscany's coastline is its extensive sandy beaches, rugged cliffs, and clean seas. Throughout the summer, tourists may enjoy swimming, tanning, and water sports in the warm and welcoming Tyrrhenian Sea. The coast is also home to numerous lovely towns and villages, including the quaint fishing hamlet of Porto Santo Stefano and the ancient port city of Livorno.

Apuan Alps National Park, which is well-known for its magnificent mountain scenery and marble quarries, is one of the most beautiful natural parks in Tuscany. Visitors may go hiking, rock climbing, mountain biking, skiing, and snowboarding in the summer and enjoy the park's many unique plant and animal species in the winter.

Another well-liked site for those who like the outdoors is the Maremma Regional Park, which has a variety of landscapes, including rocky shorelines, sandy beaches, rolling hills, and thick woods. Many endangered species, like as the European otter and the Corsican red deer, may be found in the park, and guests can enjoy cycling, hiking, and birding along its various routes.

The hot springs in Tuscany are also well-known for their medicinal benefits dating back to ancient times. Several spa towns, such as Montecatini Terme and Saturnia, which provide a variety of spa services and thermal baths, are located in the area.

In conclusion, Tuscany's natural landscapes are both varied and gorgeous, providing tourists with a broad selection of experiences and activities. Tuscany is a location with an abundance of breathtaking natural beauty, from the gently sloping hills and vineyards of the Chianti area to the jagged coastline of the Tyrrhenian Sea.

Environment and Geography

Tuscany is a region in central Italy, bounded to the north by Liguria, to the east by Emilia-Romagna, by Umbria, and to the south by Lazio. It has a population of over 3.7 million and a land area of about 23,000 square kilometers. With a variety of landscapes and weather patterns that are influenced by Tuscany's position and terrain, its geography and climate are diversified.

Geography

From the Apennine Alps to the Tyrrhenian Sea, several hills and mountain ranges make up the majority of Tuscany. The hills are distinguished by their undulating topography, which is covered with olive groves, vineyards, and fields of wheat and sunflowers. Several of Tuscany's towns and cities, such as Florence, Siena, and Pisa, have a stunning background provided by the hills.

Another noteworthy geographical feature of Tuscany is the Apennine Mountains, which stretch from the Ligurian Sea in the northwest to the Adriatic Sea in the southeast. The range has several summits that rise beyond 2,000 meters, such as Mount Falterona, and Mount Amiata. The Foreste Casentinesi National Park and the Apuan Alps National Park are only two of the national parks that can be found in the mountains.

A 400-kilometer stretch of craggy cliffs and sandy beaches make up Tuscany's coastline. Throughout the summer, tourists may enjoy swimming, tanning, and water sports in the warm and welcoming Tyrrhenian Sea. The shoreline is also home to various small fishing villages and beach towns, including Castiglioncello, Marina di Grosseto, and Porto Santo Stefano.

Climate

The climate of Tuscany is Mediterranean, with hot, dry summers and warm, wet winters. The area has a variety of microclimates, with location, height, and closeness to the sea all having an impact on the climate. With greater rainfall and lower summertime temperatures than inland locations, coastal places are often milder than inland ones.

Tuscany's summers are often hot and dry, with temperatures between 30°C and 35°C. Visitors swarm to the beaches and coastal towns in droves because of the pleasant weather, which makes it a popular time to go to the area. Throughout the summer, tourists also like visiting the interior regions to see the hill villages and wineries.

Tuscany has warm, wet winters with temperatures between 5°C and 10°C. Snowfall is a possibility on occasion in the area, especially at higher altitudes in the Apennine Mountains. In general, the winter season is calmer than the summer, with fewer visitors and a slower pace of life.

With milder weather and fewer tourists than in the summer, spring, and autumn are great periods to visit Tuscany. The hills are covered with wildflowers and the vineyards come to life in the spring, which is a particularly lovely time of year. With the grape harvest in full flow and the countryside blazing with fall colors, the fall is also a very popular season to travel.

In conclusion, Tuscany has a variety of landscapes and weather patterns that are influenced by its terrain and geographic position. The region's towns and cities are set against stunning backdrops of rolling hills and mountain ranges, and travelers seeking sunlight, mild weather, and picturesque landscapes love to come due to the region's Mediterranean climate.

CHAPTER2: GETTING THERE AND AROUND IN TUSCANY

Visa requirements

Tuscany is a stunning area in central Italy that is well-known for its magnificent scenery, fine art, rich history, and wine. Tourists from all over the globe, including the United States, like visiting it. You must be aware of various visa restrictions if you are a US visitor considering a trip to Tuscany.

Visitor Visa Requirements for Americans

The duration and purpose of the trip determine whether US visitors need a visa. You do not require a visa if you want to visit Italy for tourist, business, or transit for no more than 90 days. Alternatively, you may enter Italy using a current US passport that is good for at least three more months than the length of your intended trip.

Along with having enough money to cover your expenses while you're in Italy, you also need a ticket home or to your next stop. It's also crucial to keep in mind that you could be required to provide documentation of your lodging, such as a hotel reservation or an invitation letter from a host in Italy.

You may need a visa if you want to remain in Italy for more than 90 days or if your trip is not for business, tourism, or transit. Your reason for visiting determines the sort of visa you need. For instance, a visa that is distinct from a tourist visa is required if you want to study or work in Italy.

Italian visa types

Italian visas come in a variety of forms, including:

The most popular form of visa for tourists and business visitors who want to remain in Italy for less than 90 days is the Schengen Visa. It enables travel within the Schengen region, which comprises the majority of the nations in Europe.

If you want to remain in Italy for more than 90 days or if your visit is not for business, tourism, or transit, you must get a national visa. It is legitimate for a certain time frame and purpose, such as education or employment.

If you are passing through an Italian airport in transit and need to exit the airport's international transit area, you must have this visa.

If you are passing through Italy on your route to another nation and need to exit the international terminal of an Italian airport, you must have a transit visa.

Methods for Obtaining an Italian Visa

You must do the following actions to apply for an Italian visa:

Based on the duration of your stay and the purpose of your trip, choose the kind of visa you need.

Collect the necessary paperwork, including your passport, the visa application form, your passport images, and evidence of your ability to pay.

Set up a meeting with the Italian embassy or consulate in your home country.

Attend the appointment, then turn in your paperwork and application.

Pay the visa fee, which varies according to your nationality and the kind of visa you are applying for.

A few weeks may pass while the embassy or consulate processes your application.

In case your application is accepted, pick up your passport and visa.

It's crucial to apply for your Italian visa well in advance of the dates you want to go so that it has enough time to be processed.

Depending on their nationality, intended purpose of travel, and duration of stay, non-US persons who wish to visit Tuscany must get a visa. Italy, like many other nations, maintains a list of nations whose people are excluded from the need for a visa for transitory stays. These nations either have a visa waiver agreement with the European Union or are a member of the Schengen Area.

These nationals don't need a visa to go to Italy, including Tuscany, for up to 90 days:

member nations of the European Union
Liechtenstein, Switzerland, Norway, Iceland
South Korea, Australia, Canada, Japan, New Zealand, and the United States
Depending on the purpose and duration of your stay, you may need to apply for a Schengen Visa or a National Visa if you are a citizen of a nation not included on the list of nations for which visas are not required. Whereas the National Visa permits you to remain in Italy for more than 90 days or certain objectives like employment or study, the Schengen Visa only allows you to travel throughout the Schengen Area for up to 90 days.

You must speak with the Italian embassy or consulate in your country of residency to apply for a Schengen or National Visa and provide the necessary paperwork, which typically consists of:

- A finished visa application
- A current passport
- 2 photographs the size of a passport
- Travel documentation, such as airline tickets and hotel bookings
- Evidence of having enough money for your stay
- Travel protection that includes medical and emergency evacuation costs
- An invitation letter, if appropriate

Applying for a visa might take several weeks, so you should do it well in advance of your intended trip. Depending on your nationality and the kind of visa you need, different fees apply.

In conclusion, the visa requirements for visitors to Tuscany vary according to their country, the intended reason for travel, and the duration of stay. Although some people need a Schengen or National Visa, US citizens and nationals of a few other nations may travel to Italy for up to 90 days without one. To guarantee smooth and trouble-free travel to Tuscany, it's crucial to get in touch with the Italian embassy or consulate in your home country and follow the visa application procedure.

Transportation Options In Tuscany

Central Italy's Tuscany is a stunning area famed for its undulating hills, wineries, and quaint ancient villages. You may travel throughout Tuscany using a variety of modes of transportation if you're a tourist. I'll go through all of your alternatives for getting about in this article, including trains, buses, car rentals, taxis, and bicycles.

Trains: In Tuscany, trains are an economical and effective means of transportation. Santa Maria Novella, Florence's primary railway station, serves as the region's transportation center for all trains coming into and leaving the city. Siena, Pisa, Lucca, and Arezzo are just a few of the towns and cities in Tuscany that may be reached by the Trenitalia and Italo trains. The cost of the train varies according to the distance, kind, and time of day. Tickets may often be bought at the railway station or online. San Giovanni Valdarno, one of Tuscany's smallest railway stations, is a fantastic choice for travelers vacationing in the Chianti area.

Buses: Other means of transportation for visitors to Tuscany are buses. You may take a bus from Florence's main bus station to several cities in Tuscany, including Siena, San Gimignano, and Volterra, which is close to the Santa Maria Novella railway station. The smaller towns and villages of Tuscany are also served by several private bus operators. The cost of a bus ride depends on the route taken and the bus company you choose. Tickets may be bought at the bus station or online.

Hiring a vehicle is a common means of transportation for visitors to Tuscany since it gives you the freedom to see the area at your speed. Either the airport or the city center provides automobile rentals. Hertz, Europcar, and Avis are a few of the well-known vehicle rental businesses. It's crucial to keep in mind that driving in Tuscany might be difficult owing to the region's winding, narrow roads and the lack of parking in some of the smaller towns. Also, particularly during the busiest travel season, driving through city centers might be backed up. As a result, it's essential to exercise caution and get acquainted with the rules of the road in your area.

Taxis: For those who wish to see the area without the inconvenience of driving, taxis are a useful mode of transportation. Taxis are readily available in city centers, airport terminals, and railway stations. It's crucial to remember that taxi prices vary depending on the route taken, the hour of the day, and the firm you use. Also, before beginning your trip, it's advised to come to an agreement on a fee with the driver.

Bicycles: Cycling is a pleasant and environmentally responsible way to see the scenery of Tuscany. The larger cities, such as Florence, Siena, and Lucca, all have several bike rental shops. Depending on your inclination, you may hire a bicycle for a day or a week. If you prefer to travel the area on a bike with a local guide, there are also several guided bike excursions available.

In conclusion, travelers may travel to Tuscany using a variety of modes of transportation, including trains, buses, rental cars, taxis, and bicycles. It's important to choose the form of transportation that best meets your requirements and tastes since each has benefits and drawbacks. You're sure to find the ideal method to see Tuscany's lovely villages, gorgeous scenery, and delectable food with so many alternatives at your disposal.

Travel Tips And Guides

Central Italy's Tuscany is a stunning area famed for its undulating hills, wineries, and quaint ancient villages. To make your vacation to Tuscany as a visitor unforgettable, there are a few things to bear in mind. In this post, I'll discuss some vital travel advice to consider before visiting Tuscany.

Tuscany is a well-liked vacation location all year long, but the finest seasons to go are spring (April to June) and autumn (September to November). Compared to the busiest summer months, these seasons have pleasant weather and fewer visitors. To escape the peak season crowds, be sure to reserve your lodging and excursions in advance if you want to go during the summer.

Travel options: Tourists may travel about Tuscany using a variety of modes of transportation, including trains, buses, rental cars, taxis, and bicycles. It's crucial to do your study and choose the mode of transportation that best meets your requirements and financial situation. Also, purchasing your train or bus tickets in advance is advised to save time and avoid lengthy lines at the terminals.

Accommodations: There are many different types of lodging available in Tuscany, including hotels, bed & breakfasts, agriturismos, and villas. It is advised to reserve your lodging in advance, particularly during the busiest time of year. To have quick access to the main attractions and transit alternatives, think about staying in a central area like Florence or Siena.

Food and Drink: World-famous wines and delectable food are trademarks of Tuscany. Pasta meals like pappardelle al cinghiale (wild boar ragù), crostini toscani (chicken liver pâté), and bistecca alla fiorentina are a few of the well-liked dishes to try (Florentine steak). Moreover, Tuscany is the location of major wine-producing areas, including Montalcino, Montepulciano, and Chianti. To see the vineyards and taste some of the greatest wines in the area, think about going on a wine tour.

Italian is the official language of Italy, and learning a few fundamental words can help you interact with the people. It's also a good idea to familiarize yourself with the art, architecture, and customs of Tuscany before visiting since the area has a fascinating history and culture. For instance, to view some of the most well-known Renaissance art in the world, go to Florence's Uffizi Gallery.

Tourists may feel comfortable traveling in Tuscany, but it's still important to exercise care. For instance, remain aware of your surroundings and refrain from carrying valuables or big amounts of cash. Also, it's encouraged to select reliable transportation firms and avoid employing illegal taxis or drivers.

Dress Code: It is advised to wear proper attire while visiting the museums and places of worship in Tuscany. For instance, while visiting churches and cathedrals, shoulders and knees should be covered. Also, it is advised to wear comfortable shoes since some of the towns have cobblestone streets and steep slopes.

Tipping: While it's not customary to give a tip at restaurants in Italy, it's usual to do so if you get very good service. Checking to see whether the service fee is already included in the statement is also advised.

Etiquette: While visiting Tuscany, it's important to be considerate of the regional traditions and manners. For instance, it is considered rude to talk aloud in front of others or to cut someone off in the middle of a sentence. Also, while entering a store or restaurant, it's polite to smile and say "Buongiorno" (good morning) or "buonasera" (good evening). While speaking with locals, it's customary to say "Grazie" (I'm grateful) and "prego" (You're welcome).

CHAPTER 3: TOP CITIES AND TOP ATTRACTIONS IN TUSCANY

Tuscany is a magnificent area in central Italy known for its breathtaking scenery, extensive history, and delectable food. In this chapter, we'll look at some of the best Tuscany cities and tourist destinations.

Best Tuscany Destinations:

Florence

Tuscany's main city, Florence, is renowned for its illustrious past, exquisite works of art, and gorgeous architecture. The Florence Cathedral, the Uffizi Museum, the Ponte Vecchio, and the Palazzo Vecchio are a few of Florence's prominent tourist destinations. The Boboli Gardens and the Bardini Gardens are only two of the lovely gardens in the city that tourists may visit.

Siena

Known for its breathtaking architecture, lovely piazzas, and extensive history, Siena is a charming medieval city in Tuscany. The Piazza del Campo, the Siena Cathedral, the Palazzo Pubblico, and the Museo dell'Opera Metropolitana are just a few of Siena's prominent tourist destinations.

Pisa

Pisa is a stunning city in Tuscany known for its famed leaning tower. The iconic Leaning Tower, the Pisa Cathedral, and the Baptistery of St. John are all located in the Piazza dei Miracoli, which is open to visitors visiting Pisa. The Museo delle Sinopie and the Museo Nazionale di San Matteo are just two of the city's stunning museums.

Luca

Tuscany's picturesque city of Lucca is renowned for its exquisite architecture, breathtaking gardens, and extensive history. The Guinigi Tower, the Lucca Cathedral, and the Piazza dell'Anfiteatro are a few of Lucca's prominent tourist destinations. The lovely parks and botanical gardens that surround the city are also open to visitors.

Arezzo:

Arezzo is a lovely city in Tuscany that is renowned for its spectacular architecture, lovely churches, and rich history. The Piazza Grande, the Basilica di San Francesco, and the House Vasari are a few of Arezzo's prominent sights. Also accessible to visitors is the city's picturesque surrounding landscape.

San Gimignano

In the center of Tuscany sits the charming medieval village of San Gimignano. San Gimignano is a city rich in history, culture, and art that is well-known for its breathtaking old center. The renowned Plaza della Libertà is open to visitors.

Cisterna

Cisterna is a lovely plaza encircled by ancient structures and towers from the Middle Ages. The Collegiate Church of Santa Maria Assunta, a gorgeous church with breathtaking paintings and a lovely marble altar, is one of the other must-see attractions in San Gimignano.

Montepulciano

Southern Tuscany is home to the lovely hilltop village of Montepulciano. Montepulciano, known for its exquisite Renaissance architecture and mouth watering wine, is a charming city. Explore the majestic Palace Comunale, a magnificent Renaissance palace, which is located in the well-known Piazza Grande, a lovely plaza. Additional must-see attractions in Montepulciano include the Cathedral of Santa Maria Assunta, an elegant church with a lovely façade and complex artwork, and the Temple of San Biagio, an elegant chapel with outstanding Renaissance architecture that is situated just outside the town.

Cortona

Eastern Tuscany is home to the lovely hilltop town of Cortona. Cortona is a charming, picturesque city known for its breathtaking vistas and lovely old core. Explore the majestic Palace Comunale, a magnificent Renaissance palace, which is located in the well-known Piazza della Repubblica, a lovely plaza. The Cathedral of Santa Maria Assunta, a majestic cathedral with an exquisite façade and rich artwork, and the Etruscan Museum, which houses a collection of items from the historic Etruscan civilization, are two more must-see attractions in Cortona.

Volterra

Western Tuscany is home to the picturesque hilltop village of Volterra. Volterra is a city rich in history and culture, famous for its stunning Etruscan and Roman ruins. The majestic medieval palace, Palazzo dei Priori, is located in the well-known Piazza dei Priori, a lovely plaza. The Roman Theatre, a first-century AD antique theater with excellent preservation, and the Etruscan Museum, which houses a collection of relics from the prehistoric Etruscan culture, are two other must-see attractions in Volterra.

The Best Attractions in Tuscany

Tower Of Pisa

The Leaning Tower of Pisa is one of the most well-known structures in Italy and a must-see sight for tourists traveling to Tuscany. The tower's summit may be reached by visitors, who can then gaze out over the city and the surrounding countryside.

The Uffizi Gallery

The Uffizi Gallery is one of the most renowned art museums in the world and is where you can find a fantastic collection of Renaissance artwork. Famous painters including Botticelli,

Michelangelo, and Leonardo da Vinci have works on display for visitors to see.

Tuscany Countryside:
One of the most breathtaking natural settings on earth, the Tuscan Countryside is a must-see destination for tourists traveling to Tuscany. The gorgeous scenery of the area may be explored by tourists, who can also stroll through the picturesque vineyards, olive orchards, and rolling hills.

Florence Cathedral

The Florence Cathedral, usually referred to as the Duomo, is one of Florence's most well-known structures and a must-see site for tourists. For breathtaking views of the city and surroundings, visitors may go to the dome's summit.

The Piazza del Campo is Siena's central plaza and is renowned for its exquisite architecture, magnificent fountains, and extensive history. Tourists may stroll about the area and check out all of the nearby eateries, cafés, and stores.

The Palazzo Vecchio is a historic palace in Florence that has been the town hall of the city since the fourteenth century. Explore the palace's several chambers and take in the stunning paintings and artwork that adorn the walls.

The Boboli Gardens are a stunning garden in Florence that is situated behind the Pitti Palace. The gardens provide breathtaking views of the city as well as lovely fountains, statues, and well-kept grass.

The Chianti Wine Region: Located in the heart of Tuscany, the Chianti wine area is renowned for its mouthwatering wines, stunning vineyards, and quaint towns. Tourists may visit the many attractive towns and villages that dot the landscape or join a wine tour and enjoy some of the region's well-known wines.

The town hall of Siena is located in the ancient Palazzo Pubblico, which has been around since the 14th century. Explore the palace's several chambers and take in the stunning paintings and artwork that adorn the walls.

The San Gimignano Towers: San Gimignano is a stunning Tuscany medieval town known for its several turrets. Explore the town and take in the gorgeous architecture, or scale one of the towers for breathtaking views of the surrounding landscape.

The Cathedral of Santa Maria del Fiore is a majestic church in Florence that is well-known for its magnificent dome, which was created by Brunelleschi. Visitors may visit the cathedral's several chapels and take in the stunning wall art that adorns them.

The Ponte Vecchio is a well-known ancient bridge in Florence that is home to a large number of jewelry stores. Tourists may take a leisurely walk over the bridge, peruse the shops, and take in the stunning views of the Arno River.

The Pieta by Michelangelo and the Magdalene by Donatello are two of Florence's most well-known pieces of art, both of which are housed at the Museum dell'Opera del Duomo. The several galleries of the museum are open for visitors to explore and take in the stunning artwork on show.

The Basilica of San Francesco is a lovely church in Arezzo and is well-known for its magnificent murals by Piero della Francesca. Guests are welcome to wander the church and take in the stunning wall art.

The Medici Villas are a collection of exquisite homes dotted over Tuscany that were constructed by the illustrious Medici family. Guests are welcome to tour the homes and take in their exquisite interior decorations and architecture.

In conclusion, Tuscany is a lovely area in central Italy that is home to mouthwatering food, fascinating history, and beautiful scenery. There is always something fresh and fascinating to discover in Tuscany, whether you are exploring the lovely cities of Florence, Siena, Pisa, Lucca, and Arezzo or admiring the region's top attractions like the Leaning Tower of Pisa, the Uffizi Gallery, the Tuscan countryside, or the numerous historic palaces, churches, and museums.

CHAPTER 4: CULINARY EVENTS, TOP HOTELS, AND RESTAURANTS, FOOD, WINES

The central Italian region of Tuscany is renowned for its stunning scenery, storied towns, and top-notch cuisine and wine. The finest of Tuscany will be examined in this book, along with its renowned foods, greatest vineyards, culinary festivals, top hotels, and restaurants.

Food

High-quality meats, vegetables, and bread are the mainstays of Tuscan cuisine, which is centered on straightforward, seasonal ingredients. The following are some of the most well-known foods you may eat in Tuscany:

Ribollita
A hearty Tuscan soup called ribollita is created with bread, beans, and veggies. It is often cooked using leftover bread that has been soaked in broth until it softens. Onions, carrots, celery,

and tomatoes are then added. To give the soup a creamy texture, cannellini beans are also used. Typically, Ribollita is served with a drizzle of olive oil and some grated Parmesan cheese on top.

Steak with a Florentine sauce

The king of all steaks, or bistecca alla Fiorentina, is a renowned Tuscan steak. It is prepared with Chianina cow meat, which is renowned for its taste and suppleness. Only salt and pepper are used to season the steak while it is grilled over an open flame. With roasted potatoes or Tuscan beans, it is often served rare or medium-rare.

Cooking with pomodoro

Tuscan cuisine is known for its hearty tomato and bread soup, known as pappa al pomodoro. Olive oil, fresh tomatoes, garlic, basil, and stale bread are the ingredients. The tomato sauce is absorbed in the bread to make it soft and thick, giving the soup a creamy texture. Pappa al

Pomodoro is a well-liked summertime meal that is normally served hot or cold.

Panzanella

Stale bread, fresh tomatoes, onions, cucumbers, and basil are the main ingredients in the cooling Italian salad known as panzanella. After being soaked in water to soften, the bread is mixed with the other ingredients and seasoned with red wine vinegar and olive oil. During the summer, panzanella is a well-liked meal that is often served as a side dish or an appetizer.

Cacciucco

A variety of fish and shellfish are used to make the traditional Tuscan seafood stew called cacciucco. It is often prepared with tomatoes, garlic, and red pepper flakes and is served with a piece of toasted bread. On the Tuscan coast, cacciucco is a well-liked meal that is often served with a glass of white wine.

Wine

Chianti, Brunello di Montalcino, and Vino Nobile di Montepulciano are just a few of the top Italian wines produced in Tuscany. Some of the best wineries to visit in Tuscany are listed below:

Château Banfi
The family-run Castello Banfi winery is situated in the center of the Brunello di Montalcino area. It is renowned for producing excellent Sangiovese wines in addition to many other varietals. The vineyard has a restaurant that provides conventional Tuscan fare, as well as excursions and tastings available.

One of Tuscany's oldest and most prestigious wineries is Antinori Antinori. It was established in 1385 and is now run by a family. The winery's Chianti Class is well-known.

The Tenuta of Ornellaia

A renowned winery called Tenuta dell'Ornellaia is situated in Tuscany's Bolgheri area. The Ornellaia, Masseto, and Le Serre Nuove are among the greatest Super Tuscan wines that it is renowned for making. The vineyard has a restaurant that provides fine dining as well as guided tours and tastings.

Factory of the Barbs

The old winery Fattoria dei Barbi is situated in the center of the Brunello di Montalcino area. It is renowned for its conventional winemaking methods, which the Barbi family has been using for many years. The vineyard has a restaurant that serves traditional Tuscan fare, as well as excursions and tastings available.

Casa di Ama Castle

In the center of the Chianti Classico area sits the stunning winery Castello di Ama. It is renowned for its dedication to sustainability and the use of organic and biodynamic winemaking techniques.

The winery has a restaurant that provides fine dining as well as tours and samples available.

Food Festivals

Every year, several food festivals are held throughout Tuscany. These are some of the best festivals to check out:

Fair of the Tartufo (Truffle Fair)
The village of San Miniato hosts the Fiera del Tartufo, an annual truffle fair, in November. A truffle market, culinary demonstrations, and tastings are all part of the fair's white truffle theme.

Expo Chianti Classico
An annual wine festival called the Chianti Classico Expo takes place in September in Greve in Chianti. The festival offers local vineyards' Chianti Classico wine tastings together with food vendors, live music, and cultural activities.

Summer Festival in Lucca

An annual music event called the Lucca Summer Festival takes place in the city of Lucca in July. International performers play during the event, and there are also food and drink sellers.

Siena's Palio

An annual horse race called the Palio di Siena takes place in Siena during July and August. A celebration with food, wine, and music is held after the race and is preceded by a procession of characters dressed in costumes.

Artigiano Bacco

The Bacco Artigiano wine festival is held in May in the town of Montepulciano. Vino Nobile di Montepulciano wine tastings from nearby vineyards are offered during the festival, along with food vendors and cultural activities.

Best Hotels

There are several well-regarded hotels in Tuscany, from opulent resorts to little bed & breakfasts. The best hotels to take into account are listed below:

Castle di Casole at Belmond
Amid the Tuscan countryside, Belmond Castle di Casole is a luxurious hotel housed in a 10th-century castle that has been rebuilt. The hotel has a spa, an infinity pool, and a variety of restaurants, including one that serves conventional Tuscan fare.

Salviatino, Il
Just outside of Florence, in a 15th-century house that has been rebuilt, there is a five-star hotel called Il Salviatino. The hotel has a spa, an outdoor swimming pool, and a fine dining restaurant.

Castle of the Nero

In the center of the Chianti Classico area, Castle del Nero is a luxurious hotel housed in a 12th-century castle that has been rebuilt. The hotel has a spa, an outdoor swimming pool, and a restaurant serving typical Tuscan fare.

Santo Pietro, Borgo
At a 13th-century house that has been refurbished close to Siena, there is a premium boutique hotel called Borgo Santo Pietro. The hotel has a spa, an outdoor swimming pool, and a restaurant that offers farm-to-table food produced with ingredients that are obtained locally.

Castiglion del Bosco Rosewood
Rosewood In the center of the Val d'Orcia area, Castiglion del Bosco is a luxurious hotel housed in a 17th-century mansion that has been rebuilt. The hotel has a spa, an outdoor swimming pool, and a restaurant serving typical Tuscan fare.

Top Restaurants

Some of Italy's top dining establishments may be found in Tuscany, where they provide regionally produced classic Tuscan dishes. These are a few of the best eateries to take into account:

Osteria Francescana
Around an hour's drive from Florence, in the city of Modena, lies the three-Michelin-star Osteria Francescana. The eatery is renowned for its creative food, which combines contemporary cooking methods with classic Italian tastes.

The Buon Caffè Shop
In the center of Florence, there is a Michelin-starred restaurant called La Bottega del Buon Caffè. The eatery provides seasonal Tuscan cuisine cooked with ingredients acquired locally and has a patio with views of the Arno River.

Passignano's Restaurant

A 30-minute drive from Florence, in the Chianti Classico area, sits the Michelin-starred restaurant Osteria di Passignano. The eatery is well-known for its home-cooked pasta dishes and grilled meats that are served with regional wines.

Los Tendaros

In the village of Greve in Chianti, there is a family-run restaurant called La Tenda Rossa. The eatery is renowned for its vast wine list and the authentic Tuscan fare including wild boar stew and handmade ravioli.

The Buca di Monte

At San Gimignano, there is a family-run eatery called La Buca di Montauto. The eatery is well-known for its home-cooked pasta, roasted meats, and regional wines that are served in a welcoming setting.

In conclusion, Tuscany is a place that provides lovers of food and wine with a distinctive and wonderful experience. There is something for every kind of tourist, from famous wines and restaurants to lovely bed & breakfasts and cultural events. Tuscany is undoubtedly a place not to be missed because of its breathtaking scenery, extensive history, and world-class food.

CHAPTER 5: TRAVEL TIPS

Accomodations

One of the most popular tourist destinations in Italy is Tuscany, which is known for its extensive history, breathtaking scenery, and top-notch food. As a result, there are several lodging alternatives for visitors to the area, from opulent hotels to lovely bed & breakfasts. We'll provide a general overview of the many kinds of lodging available in Tuscany in this guide and highlight some of the top choices in each category.

Hotels: The most common kind of lodging in Tuscany is a hotel, which provides a broad variety of alternatives to fit every taste and budget. Tuscany offers everything, from opulent five-star hotels to reasonably priced accommodations. Several hotels in Tuscany are built in old structures, such as palaces and castles, and they provide breathtaking views of the surrounding landscape. The following are a few of the top hotels in Tuscany:

Castle di Casole: This opulent hotel is located in a 10th-century castle that has been beautifully refurbished and provides breathtaking views of the Tuscan countryside. The hotel has a Michelin-starred restaurant, spa, and outdoor pool.

A five-star hotel with a spa, an outdoor pool, and a top-notch restaurant, the Four Seasons Hotel Firenze is situated in the center of Florence.

The five-star hotel Borgo Santo Pietro is housed in a 13th-century estate that has been refurbished and has a spa, an outdoor pool, and a Michelin-starred restaurant.

Florence's Hotel Lungarno is a five-star establishment with a Michelin-starred restaurant and spa that is situated on the banks of the Arno River.

Farmhouses or other rural properties that provide lodging to visitors are known as agriturismos. For those seeking a more genuine Tuscan experience, they are a terrific choice since they often have rustic, lovely décor and classic Tuscan food. A lot of agriturismos also provide additional activities like wine tastings and cookery workshops. In Tuscany, some of the top agriturismos are:

The Chianti region's Fattoria La Loggia is an agriturismo with a restaurant, wine cellar, and a swimming pool.

Agriturismo Podere Santa Pia: This Maremma-area inn provides culinary workshops and wine tastings together with breathtaking views of the Tuscan countryside.

The Val d'Orcia area is home to the agriturismo La Pietriccia, which has a restaurant, wine cellar, and a swimming pool.

Agriturismo El Casale del Marchese: This agriturismo is situated in the Montepulciano area and has a restaurant, wine cellar, and a swimming pool.

In Tuscany, bed and breakfasts are a popular kind of lodging because they provide a more personal, cozy atmosphere. While they sometimes have less facilities and are smaller than hotels and agriturismos, they can provide a more individualized experience. Traditional Tuscan décor may be seen at many bed and breakfasts in Tuscany that are housed in historical structures. The following are a few of the top bed and breakfasts in Tuscany:

Il Vicario is a bed & breakfast with a swimming pool and breathtaking views of the Tuscan countryside that is situated in the Chianti area.

Palazzo Malaspina: This bed and breakfast is situated in the center of Florence and has classic Tuscan design. It is set in a 15th-century palace.

The bed and breakfast known as Antica Torre di Via Tornabuoni 1 is housed in a tower that dates back to the 13th century and provides breathtaking views of Florence.

Il Pozzo di Radi is a bed & breakfast with a garden, a swimming pool, and typical Tuscan furnishings that is situated in the Val d'Elsa area.

Renting a villa or apartment in Tuscany is a fantastic choice for those searching for a more autonomous lodging option. For families or groups of friends vacationing together, villas and apartments are a terrific alternative since they provide more room and privacy than hotels or bed & breakfasts. Tuscany has a large number of old structures that house villas and apartments, many of which have breathtaking views of the surrounding landscape. The following are a few of the top homes and flats in Tuscany:

Villa le Barone is a property with a swimming pool, gardens, and breathtaking views of the Tuscan countryside. It is situated in the Chianti area.

La Torre del Cielo: This apartment is in Florence's historic district and has breathtaking views of the city's iconic buildings.

Villa Montecastello: This property, which is situated in the Montepulciano area, has a swimming pool, gardens, and typical Tuscan furnishings.

Borgo Finocchieto is a property with a swimming pool, gardens, and breathtaking views of the Tuscan countryside that is situated in the Val d'Orcia area.

Camping is a terrific choice in Tuscany for those seeking a more adventurous kind of lodging. There are several camping alternatives available in Tuscany, from budget-friendly campgrounds to exclusive resorts. Camping is a more cost-effective choice than hotels or villas and is a wonderful way to enjoy the area's breathtaking nature. The following are a few of the top camping areas in Tuscany:

The Chianti region's Campsite Village Il Poggetto is a campground with a restaurant, swimming pools, and breathtaking views of the Tuscan landscape.

The San Gimignano region's Campsite Boschetto di Piemma has a restaurant, a swimming pool, and rustic Tuscan furnishings.

Free Time Camping Village: This campground has a café, a swimming pool, and convenient access to the sea in the Maremma area.

The Montepulciano area's Campsite La Chiocciola is a campground with a restaurant, a swimming pool, and typical Tuscan furnishings.

In conclusion, Tuscany provides a variety of lodging choices to fit every need and preference. Tuscany offers a variety of lodging options, including opulent hotels, rustic agriturismos, lovely bed & breakfasts, roomy villas and apartments, and reasonably priced campsites. Tuscany is the ideal vacation spot for anybody seeking an exceptional Italian experience because of its fascinating history, breathtaking scenery, and top-notch food.

Culture And Language

One of the most well-liked tourist locations in Italy is Tuscany. It is renowned for its beautiful scenery, extensive history, and vibrant art and culture. To navigate and fully enjoy your journey as a tourist, it is essential to have some familiarity with the regional language and culture. This book will provide a general introduction of Tuscany's language and culture, including topics like vocabulary, popular expressions, regional customs and traditions, food, and more.

Initial Language

Together with Italian, Tuscan is a regional tongue spoken in Tuscany. Roman, Germanic, and other languages have impacted the language's evolution throughout time. Famous authors like Dante, Petrarch, and Boccaccio all spoke a dialect of Italian known as the Tuscan dialect, which is sometimes regarded as the purest variety of the language.

Despite the fact that Italian is the country's official language, Tuscan is still extensively spoken throughout Tuscany, especially in the countryside. Although younger generations are more likely to be multilingual in Italian and Tuscan, many elderly individuals still solely speak Tuscan.

To converse with people and demonstrate respect for the language and culture, travelers should learn a few fundamental Tuscan words. These are some typical Tuscan phrases:

Buongiorno Happy morning!
Buonasera (Good evening)

How are you? How are you doing?

Grazie (Thank you)

(Yes) Si (No)

Thank you (Please)

Scusa (Pardon me)

I'm sorry. (Pardon, formal)

Culture

Due to its history and location, Tuscany has a rich and varied cultural legacy. The following are some intriguing facets of Tuscan culture that travelers could enjoy:

Tuscany is home to some of the most well-known pieces of art and architecture in the whole world. With sculptures like Michelangelo's David and Botticelli's The Birth of Venus, Florence, the capital of Tuscany, is renowned as the cradle of the Renaissance. Cities like Pisa, Siena, and Lucca are home to further noteworthy masterpieces.

Christianity is the most prevalent religion in Tuscany, which has a significant religious heritage. There are other stunning churches and cathedrals in the area, including the Duomo in Florence and the Cathedral of Siena. The whole year is filled with religious celebrations and processions, such as the Palio di Siena, a horse race conducted in the city's main piazza.

Tuscany food is renowned for its simplicity and use of natural, regional ingredients. Other well-known foods include pappa al pomodoro, bistecca alla fiorentina, and ribollita (a robust vegetable soup) (a tomato and bread soup). Wine from Tuscany is very well-known, especially Chianti and Brunello di Montalcino.

Tuscany has a long history of regional festivals and customs, many of which are connected to religion or agriculture. The grape harvest, which takes place in the autumn and entails gathering and processing grapes to produce wine, is one noteworthy custom. Additional celebrations include the Giostra del Carnevale, a bustling march in Viareggio, and the Carnival of Viareggio.

Arezzo hosts the Saracino, a medieval jousting competition.

Fashion and design: Florence and other Tuscan towns are home to a number of renowned fashion businesses and designers that have a long history in the industry. High-end textiles and apparel are also quite popular, as are leather products like purses and shoes.

Although Tuscans are mostly amiable and welcoming, it is nevertheless vital for visitors to observe proper social behavior. For instance, depending on the degree of familiarity, it is common to greet individuals with a handshake or a kiss on both cheeks. It's also crucial to dress correctly, especially while visiting churches or other places of worship. Although giving a tip is not as customary in Italy as it is in some other nations, doing so is still appreciated.

Conclusion:

Tourists interested in history, art, culture, and gastronomy should visit Tuscany. While Italian is the country's official language, knowing a few simple words in the local dialect may help tourists interact with residents and appreciate their way of life. Tuscany has a rich and varied cultural legacy, which includes food, fashion, design, religion, art and architecture, as well as local customs and traditions. Tourists may improve their experience and have a greater understanding of this stunning area of Italy by learning about these facets of Tuscan culture.

Money Issues

This is a handbook that explains all the information you need about money, exchange rates, ATMs, credit cards, and more.

Tuscany's currency

The Euro (€) is the currency used in Tuscany and all of Italy. There are 100 pennies in one euro. Coins are available in the following denominations: 1, 2, 5, 10, 20, and 50 cents, as well as €1 and €2. Notes are available in the following denominations: €5, €10, €20, €50, €100, €200, and €500.

Rates of exchange

Before coming to Tuscany, it is advisable to verify the current currency rate since they might vary rapidly. To acquire the most recent rates, you may check the exchange rate online or using an app like XE Currency or Currency Converter Plus. Remember that the exchange rate you get in a currency exchange office may differ from the one you see online.

Money Exchange

Banks, currency exchange companies, and certain hotels all provide currency exchange services. The best exchange rates are often provided by banks, however there may be a commission or flat cost for the transaction.

Another option is to use a currency exchange office, although they often have worse rates and more expensive fees. Be aware that the rates at a hotel may not be as good as those at a bank or foreign exchange office if you decide to convert money there.

ATMs

In Tuscany, there are many ATMs, making them a practical option to receive cash. The majority of ATMs accept Visa, Mastercard, and Maestro along with other popular credit and debit cards. ATMs are often located at banks, post offices, retail establishments, and tourist destinations. To avoid ATM fees, check with your bank before you go to see if they have any relationships with banks in Italy. Be in mind that certain ATMs may charge a fee for withdrawals. In order to prevent any problems with your card being banned, make sure to let your bank know about your vacation intentions as well.

Credit Cards

In Tuscany, particularly in the busier tourist destinations and bigger towns, credit cards are routinely accepted. The most widely used credit cards are Visa and Mastercard, however American Express is also accepted at select locations. While it's always a good idea to have some extra cash on hand, using a credit card to pay for things like meals, lodging, and attractions may be easy and secure.

Tipping
While it's less customary than in some other nations, tipping is nevertheless expected for excellent service in Italy. At restaurants, cafés, and bars, it's customary to round up the bill or leave a tiny bit of change as a tip. While it's not customary, you may leave a higher tip if you're really happy with the service. Another custom in hotels is to give the housekeeping workers a little gratuity.

Taxes In Italy, the cost of the majority of products and services includes VAT. The regular VAT rate is 22%, however certain products are subject to lower rates of 10% and 4%. Non-EU citizens may get a VAT refund for items they bought in Italy and are transporting outside of the EU. You'll need to provide your passport, a filled-out tax-free form, and the genuine receipts from your transactions in order to accomplish this.

Security and Safety

Traveling in Tuscany is typically secure, but you should always be cautious with your money and possessions. Don't carry significant sums of cash on you; instead, keep your cash and credit cards in a secure location, such a money belt or a pocket. Keep a watch out for pickpockets in popular tourist locations, particularly in bigger cities like Florence. Be alert of your surroundings.

Tuscany may be an expensive travel destination, particularly during the busiest travel months. Setting a budget and making plans in advance for your vacation is a smart idea. Depending on the area and season, prices for lodging, food, and activities might vary greatly. Predictably, prices will be higher in bigger cities and popular tourist destinations like Florence and Pisa and lower in smaller towns and rural regions.

Accomodations

The location, time of year, and kind of lodging all have an impact on the cost of accommodations in Tuscany. Agriturismo lodgings, which are farmhouses transformed into guesthouses, are less expensive than hotels in bigger towns and famous tourist destinations. In certain places, you may also find affordable lodging options like hostels and guesthouses.

Depending on your mode of transportation, the cost of transportation in Tuscany might also vary greatly. While renting a vehicle might be pricey, it gives you the most freedom and is the greatest way to see the beautiful scenery of the area. While less expensive, public transportation like buses and trains may not be as handy for seeing smaller towns and rural regions. Be prepared to walk a bit since many of Tuscany's old town centers are pedestrian-only areas.

food and beverage

In Tuscany, food and drink may be rather expensive, particularly if you eat out often. Instead of going to more expensive restaurants, think about choosing one of the neighborhood trattorias and osterias. If you're staying in a self-catering facility, such as an apartment or an agriturismo, you may also save money by doing your own grocery shopping and cooking.

Activities and Attractions

There are several well-known tourist destinations in Tuscany, like the Leaning Tower of Pisa and the Uffizi Museum in Florence, although entry costs may be expensive. Consider going off-season when costs are cheaper or buying a combo ticket for many attractions if you want to save money. Free outdoor activities like hiking and touring old towns and villages are abundant, as are many smaller museums and galleries.

To sum up, Tuscany is a beautiful and diversified area that has plenty to offer all kinds of tourists. You may take advantage of everything that Tuscany has to offer without going over your budget if you are conscious of your money and set realistic goals. Keep in mind to be mindful of your surroundings, safeguard your cash and credit cards, and have fun on your vacation!

How to Be Safe in Tuscany

While Tuscany is typically a secure destination for travelers, it is nevertheless vital to take safety measures when visiting any location. These are some recommendations for being safe in Tuscany:

Watch out for pickpockets.
In Tuscany, pickpocketing is a frequent crime, particularly in popular tourist destinations. Always be mindful of your surroundings and keep your possessions near by. Think about carrying your valuables in a lockable bag or a money belt. A backup credit card, identification, and small quantities of cash should all be kept in a secure location.

While use ATMs, use care.
In Italy, ATM skimming is a rising issue, and Tuscany is not an exception. Utilize ATMs that are housed in secure facilities like banks, and cover the keypad while inputting your PIN. Before using the ATM, look for any indications of manipulation, such as a loose card reader or a camera fastened to the device.

Observe the traffic

Particularly in bigger towns like Florence, traffic in Tuscany can be a complete mess. While crossing the street, pedestrians should always utilize crosswalks and pay attention to oncoming cars. Drivers should be careful while traveling through new locations and be wary of small, curving roadways.

Beware of con artists
In Tuscany, particularly in well-known tourist destinations like Florence and Pisa, tourist frauds are rather widespread. Be aware of anybody attempting to sell you anything or giving you assistance without your permission. Avoid talking to street sellers and declining unauthorized offers of tours or other services.

On public transit, pay attention.
Although it's normally safe to use Tuscany's public transit, it's still a good idea to pay attention to your surroundings. Keep your possessions close at hand at all times, and stay away from carrying bulky bags or backpacks that might attract thieves. If possible, avoid

going alone and use caution while utilizing public transit at night.

Be ready for calamities caused by nature.
Natural calamities like earthquakes and floods are common in Tuscany. Know the weather forecast and any possible dangers in your immediate neighborhood. Consider the likelihood of landslides and floods if you're going during the rainy season, and stay away from trekking in regions that are vulnerable to these natural catastrophes.

the emergency numbers to call
It's crucial to be familiar with the local emergency numbers in case of an emergency. The emergency number for police, ambulance, and fire services in Italy is 112. Make sure someone is aware of your whereabouts at all times, and keep a copy of your passport and other critical papers in a secure location.

Be mindful of regional traditions

It's crucial to respect the regional traditions and customs since Tuscany is a conservative area. While visiting churches and other religious places, dress modestly, and when dealing with locals, be mindful of any etiquette rules that may apply. Especially at night, refrain from creating loud sounds or disturbing the serenity.

In conclusion, Tuscany is a usually safe place to visit for visitors, but it's vital to exercise care. Be mindful of your surroundings, keep your possessions close to hand, and show respect for regional traditions and customs. You may take advantage of everything Tuscany has to offer while keeping safe and secure by paying attention to these suggestions.

CONCLUSION: FINAL THOUGHTS AND RECOMMENDATIONS

Central Italy's Tuscany region is a stunning area. Rolling hills, beautiful scenery, and magnificent art centers like Florence, Pisa, and Siena are among its most well-known features. Tourists may enjoy a wide range of experiences in Tuscany, including its natural beauty, gastronomy, and wine. There are a few things you should know if you're considering a vacation to Tuscany to maximize your enjoyment of the region. We'll examine some of the crucial details you should be aware of before beginning your vacation in Tuscany in this guide.

Tuscany's Best Time to Visit
Tuscany is best visited in April through June or September through October. The weather is pleasant, and there are fewer visitors during

these months. The busiest and warmest times of year are July and August when highs of up to 35°C (95°F) are common. It is difficult to go about at this time since a lot of businesses shut down for the holidays, including restaurants and stores.

How to Navigate Tuscany

Having a vehicle is the greatest way to see all of Tuscany. Major cities like Florence, Pisa, and Siena have several automobile rental agencies. There are several different modes of transportation, however, if you'd rather not drive. Tuscany's main cities and villages are connected by trains and buses, which constitute an inexpensive mode of transportation. You may also utilize the city's public transit system, which includes buses and trams, to go about the area.

Accommodations in Tuscany

Tuscany offers a wide range of lodging choices, from opulent hotels to inexpensive hostels. You may stay in one of the numerous five-star hotels in Florence or Siena if you want an opulent experience. On the other hand, if you're on a tight budget, the area is full of hostels and guesthouses.

Things to Do and See in Tuscany
Tuscany offers a variety of sights and activities. The following are some of the top sights:

Florence: The Birth of Venus by Botticelli and Michelangelo's David are two of the most well-known pieces of art in the whole world. The Cathedral, Uffizi Gallery, and Ponte Vecchio are further points of interest worth seeing.

Pisa: The Leaning Tower, which is situated in the Piazza dei Miracoli, draws the majority of tourists to this city. The Baptistery and the Cathedral are just a few of the city's other standout features.

Siena: This city is renowned for its exquisite architecture, which includes the Torre del Mangia and the Palazzo Pubblico. The renowned Palio horse race, which is held twice a year, is also held in the city.

Chianti: This area is well-known for its wine and beautiful landscape. A wine tour or a visit to one of the numerous nearby vineyards are also options for tourists.

San Gimignano is a medieval town distinguished for its towers and winding lanes. If you're interested in history and architecture, it's a fantastic location to explore.

Lucca: This city is renowned for its still-standing Renaissance city walls. Views of the city may be seen when strolling around the walls.

Cinque Terre is a group of five settlements situated along the Ligurian Sea coast. To enjoy the breathtaking coastline, tourists may either stroll between the settlements or take a boat excursion.

Food and drink options in Tuscany

The simplicity and freshness of the ingredients used in Tuscan cooking are well-recognized. The followings are some foods and beverages you need to sample when visiting Tuscany:

Ribollita: This is a typical Tuscan vegetable and bread soup.

Pappa al Pomodoro is a traditional Tuscan meal that is created with bread, tomatoes, and olive oil.

Salt and pepper-seasoned grilled T-bone steak is known as bistecca alla Fiorentina.

Sheep's milk cheese called Pecorino is a staple of Tuscan cooking.

One of the most renowned red wines produced in Tuscany is the Chianti, a red wine created from Sangiovese grapes.

Things to Bring with You to Tuscany

It's crucial to take the season and your planned activities into account while preparing for your vacation to Tuscany. The following are some things to think about bringing:

Comfortable walking shoes are necessary since you'll probably be doing a lot of walking.

Summer temperatures may be rather hot, therefore it's necessary to have lightweight clothes. Lightweight, breathable clothing is also important.

Sunscreen: Using sunscreen may help shield your skin from the sun's damaging rays, which is particularly crucial during the summer.

Bring an adaptor if you want to use gadgets since Italy utilizes a different kind of electrical plug than many other nations.

Camera: Tuscany is a beautiful place, therefore you should use a camera to record your experiences.

Travel Safety Advice for Tuscany

Although Tuscany is normally a secure place to go, you must nevertheless take security measures to protect yourself. Observe the following safety advice:

Keep an eye out for potential dangers, particularly in busy places.

Put your valuables in a secure location and be on the lookout for pickpockets.

Be mindful of the curvy, winding roads and Italian driving habits if you're driving.

While utilizing public transit, particularly at night, use vigilance at all times.

Your trip to Tuscany would be one to remember with all these guides

A Merry Travelling To You!

Made in the USA
Monee, IL
07 April 2023

31497505R00066